Table of Contents

the
ULTIMATE COWORKING
LAUNCH SEQUENCE
interactive workbook

BY ANGEL KWIATKOWSKI
FOUNDER, COHERE COWORKING

FOREWORD

DELIVERED BY ANGEL, DETERMINED BY US: A FOUNDING MEMBER'S MUSINGS

Being an entrepreneur can be a lonely pursuit.

Related: being a human can be a lonely pursuit.

Sometimes you just need someone to help you celebrate, commiserate, collaborate, uncomplicate or recalibrate, and when you're working independently, that someone is only you. Or the UPS guy, who doesn't really have that kind of time. Believe me, I understand this because I lived this.

By 2009, I had been through 3 rounds of working from home >> moving to a private office >> working from home >> trying an executive suite situation >> working from home. I was exhausted from the pursuit of the Elusive Whatever: companionship? motivation? advice? shared snacks? occasional group laughter? Whatever it was, it was missing, and that sucked. Big time.

When I heard about a Meetup that was designed to explore the idea of something called "coworking" I thought "what the hell?" and I showed up. Luckily, other people did, too. Cohere Coworking Community was born that day, in someone else's coffee shop conference room, delivered by Angel and determined by … us. We didn't yet have a permanent home, but we had the people, and as if by magic there was companionship, motivation, advice, shared snacks and more-than-occasional group laughter. I got more done, better, and happily -- and it didn't matter if we were working from folding tables in an incubator lobby (we were at first); or whether we had a name, or a printer, or sleek Scandinavian furniture (we didn't at first); or whether we had a receptionist (we still don't, because we welcome one another).

It turns out that the Elusive Whatever is Community. It takes a willingness to show up, and share, and it's impossible to accomplish alone. It's made from people, not things, and that's what made all the difference for me, my career, and my happiness.

In this book, you'll learn why coworking is unique, the problems it can solve, and how to build a coworking community from the ground up. Not in a high-level, grandiose, requires-$100k-in-seed-funding way, but in a basic, bootstrapped, people-centered way. A way that values cooperation and collaboration, and creates a space where people can thrive while maintaining their passion for independence.

Most importantly, you'll discover how to recognize, nurture, and maintain organic community growth, a valuable skill that will encourage success as a coworking space catalyst...and beyond.

Having spent nearly 3,000 days as a member of Cohere, I can say with absolute certainty that community is the key to making coworking … work.

Julie Sutter
Founding Member, Cohere, Summer 2017

THE CAST OF CO-CREATORS

AUTHOR

Angel Kwiatkowski
Cohere Founder

Angel is the founder of Cohere, the first and largest community-managed shared office space in Fort Collins, Colorado. Since its opening in 2010, Cohere has helped more than 500 local freelancers and remote employees integrate in their community to achieve professional and personal success. Co-author of the first-ever ebooks about coworking, Angel was the token female panelist at the first-ever Global Coworking Unconference and Conference (GCUC) in 2011, and is among only a few female coworking consultants in America.

In addition to these firsts, she also founded Fort Collins' first niche collaborative rehearsal space for musicians in 2015.

Voted "Most Likely to Change the World" in high school, she confesses to being more enamored with the Junior Fire Chief post she was awarded in third grade. A failed stay-at-home mom, Angel frequently bakes cookies and brownies for Cohere's members in between taking conference calls and drum lessons. She just launched fo(co)works, a collaborative alliance of local coworking spaces (the first in Fort Collins, naturally). She has a Bachelor's degree in psychology, a Master's degree in organizational performance and change, and a certificate of participation.

Meet Angel at **www.coherecommunity.com**.

EDITOR

Beth Buczynski
Cohere Alumnus

Beth is a writer and editor who has been freelance, remote, or self-employed for the better part of 10 years. She lives with her husband and two very spoiled cats in Northern Colorado, and is proud to have been one of the founding members of Cohere. Joining the coworking community gave Beth confidence, provided new opportunities, and most importantly, allowed her to create friendships with talented people she respects and admires. Beth is the author of Sharing Is Good, a guide to the burgeoning world of collaborative consumption, and has been published by Shareable, STIR Magazine, and Utne Reader, among many others.

Get to know Beth at **www.about.me/ bethbuczynski**.

DESIGNER

Jenny Fischer
Cohere Member

Jenny's status as a type and design junkie started very early. When she was a kid, she designed a font on her parents' Apple Macintosh, using MacDraw. Totally hooked, she has been absorbing art and design ever since, and has worked as a graphic designer since entering college. Combining her love for design with an eight-year stint as a college media adviser has given her a better perspective on thinking outside of the box, a well-tested method for keeping a team on track and on deadline, and a solid sense of humor when it comes to rolling with the punches.

Jenny's favorite thing about coworking is sharing space with people who have the same passion for their jobs that she does for hers–and hearing about their projects, goals, trials, and conquests.

See Jenny's portfolio at **www.jennyfischer. com**.

DESIGNER

Becca Verna
Cohere Member

Becca is a designer and copywriter whose love of pretty things and tech began while playing with her MacPaint program in the 80s. Since then, she's created a bunch of online courses for universities and startups, and now works with creatives, makers, and business badasses to design websites, brands, and copy. Her favorite thing about coworking? The meandering, esoteric conversations about precisely nothing.

See Becca's work at **www.beccaverna.com**.

INTRODUCTION

WHAT IS COWORKING?

Coworking is a phenomenon that happens in shared, collaborative work spaces. Coworking values community (not space), relationships, and productivity. Coworking has its foundation in the freelance/self-employed industry, but has expanded to include and nurture small to moderate-sized businesses, non-profits, remote employees, consultants, and emerging industries. Read more at www. coworking.com.

Coworking is a state of mind, a family, and a revolutionary element of the larger collaborative consumption movement. But figuring out how to get the most out of this new style of working can be difficult if you don't know what it's about or where to find it. So next I'd like to talk about what coworking isn't.

WHAT COWORKING IS NOT

Coworking, at its birth and in its heart, has never been about just renting desks. It's about being part of a community-based movement that is literally changing the face of work as we know it.

I'm not here to sell you on the idea that coworking is the only way to work. Coworking isn't the end. It's the beginning. It's the road. It's the vehicle. Through coworking, you can become a better, more complete, well-rounded, balanced,

tolerant, educated, motivated citizen of the world, while realizing your personal and professional goals..and isn't that really what we're all after?

WHAT MAKES COWORKING UNIQUE?

Coworking is the answer for freelancers and other location-independent professionals who are tired of the isolation of their home office and the distraction of

> *"Coworking acknowledges the physical, emotional, and spiritual needs of the location-independent workforce by providing a community where socialization and collaboration are readily available."*

their local coffee shop.

It's easy to find free WiFi and a place to lay your laptop, but coworking provides more. It gives you access to a global community that is a support system, educational network, and creative think-tank all rolled into one. Coworking recognizes that we are social creatures who can accomplish more together than we do alone.

BENEFITS OF THE COWORKING ATMOSPHERE

In their book ReWork, Jason Fried and David Heinemeier wrote "instead of thinking about how you can land a roomful of rock stars, think about the room instead...The environment has a lot more to do with great work than most people think."

The guys from ReWork go on to say that, "there's a ton of untapped potential trapped under lame policies, poor direction, and stifling bureaucracies. Cut the crap and you'll find that people are dying to do great work. They just need to be given the chance." If you've been doubting your ability to do great work lately, maybe it's time to consider the change of scenery that coworking can provide. Find ReWork at www.37signals.com/rework.

PRIVACY/EXPOSURE

The 2017 State of Telecommuting in the U.S. Employee Workforce report found that telecommuting grew 115% in the past decade, nearly 10 times faster than the rest of the workforce, and 40 percent more employers offer flexible workspace options than they did in 2010. If you're one of these telecommuters, the way to produce a high level of work isn't to lock yourself in a home office. When you cowork, you have the opportunity to change the place, time, and style of work environment to fit your daily needs. Need to get some serious work done? Tell the community that you're having a "me" day, and retreat to the quietest corner. Need to rant about a nightmare client or brainstorm through a mental block? Your therapy/focus group is ready and waiting. See the report at http://bit.ly/2x3k4pQ.

AUTONOMY/RESPONSIBILITY

When you're working a traditional 9 to 5 job, a lack of greatness can be blamed on the boss/computer/lighting/janitor/coffee. When you're coworking, the responsibility falls on you and you alone. Giving yourself just one or two days a week to work freely on projects you're passionate about can jumpstart your productivity in ways you never imagined.

PRAISE/CONSTRUCTIVE CRITICISM

We all know what it's like to be chastised for doing something wrong, but fewer professionals know what it feels like to reap immediate praise for accomplishing something great. Coworking provides you with a community that will applaud when you finally locate a pesky coding bug, or throw a party when you launch a new

WHAT IS COWORKING?

product. Rest assured, coworkers will also tell you when an idea misses the mark, but it will be because they want you to succeed and be happy, not because they're worried about the bottom line. And speaking of finances...

COWORKING CAN SAVE YOU FROM BEING BROKE

While coworking is by no means limited to freelancers, they do make up the backbone of many communities. In fact, a 2016 survey found that around 35 percent of all U.S. workers are freelancers. So they kind of make up the backbone of the economy too. Unfortunately, one less-than-exhilarating consequence of being a freelancer is the loss of a regular paycheck. Read the survey at http://bit.ly/2xR9lCQ.

Traditional, salaried professionals know that a check will magically appear on pay day whether they worked their ass off or spent most of the week scrolling through Facebook. When you're self-employed, no work means no pay. Period. If you've recently decided to branch out on your own, you've probably already felt that deep abdominal anxiety that occurs when you bank account dips below the 'safety' level. You might think that fluctuating income means you can't afford coworking, but it's actually proof that you can't afford not to.

NEW OPPORTUNITIES

Opportunities abound in a coworking space. Whether it's bartering work with your desk neighbor, or raising your hand when someone says, "I need help upgrading my website," coworking attracts work. There's also the chance that your coworker will see an online job posting you missed, or tell you in advance that their company is looking for some remote help. If you're not there, you won't be able to take advantage of it.

ENCOURAGEMENT

You know that panic I mentioned earlier? You're not the only one who's felt it. Every freelancer or small business owner has felt that same fear, and lain awake at night wondering how they would make ends meet.

When you're part of a coworking community, you'll get free advice (OK, therapy) from experienced independents about how to budget, survive, and find new work.

Coworking allows you to share work-related fears without embarrassment or judgment.

DISTRACTION

Financial stress is the worst, but that doesn't mean you stay holed up in your home office, devoid of fun and human contact. Don't retreat, embrace it! Use your coworking community as a sounding board for ideas, attend free networking events, and schedule meetups. Relax. Laugh. Remember that you chose to be location-independent because it's what makes you happy, not because it will make you a millionaire. This too shall pass, and you'll feel amazing for sticking with your passion and making something out of what seemed like nothing.

STAGNATION

Starting a business isn't a decision to be taken lightly. Most freelancers and small business owners are so focused on keeping the bills paid, they forget how vital things like fresh air and conversation can be to their business' success.

The same principle applies for remote employees, who, while not necessarily worried about "keeping the lights on," can still suffer from the frustration and stagnation that comes from working outside an office. While emails, virtual meetings, and Slack chat can alleviate some of this isolation, they're no substitute for real conversations with real human beings.

If you (or someone you know) are hesitant to try coworking, here are some compelling reasons to experience work outside the home office:

MOTIVATION

Joining a coworking community is like having a double shot of motivation in your morning latte. It might surprise you to know that there are people who find your ideas/talents/products impressive and constantly encourage you to reach for more. They're called coworkers, and they are waiting to assure you that there is a reason to keep going.

NETWORKING

Aside from those special souls who were born for cold calling, have you ever met someone who really enjoys networking events? There's all that awkward glancing between faces and name tags, painful small talk about the catered food, and the inevitable fumbling for business cards.

When you're part of a coworking community, networking ceases to be a traumatizing event and instead becomes a natural part of your daily routine. Each day, you'll be sitting next to someone new, with a whole set of talents, resources, and connections waiting to be shared.

WHAT IS COWORKING?

BARTERING

Money tight? Working in a community of small business owners and freelancers means that everyone can relate. But instead of breaking down, coworkers barter. Chances are, within 20 feet of your laptop, you'll find someone who's willing to trade web design work for some help with marketing, or new headshots in exchange for a keyword-optimized blog post.

OUTSOURCING

On the flip side, if you've got more work than you can handle, there's no need to give up sleep or force your family into indentured servitude. As a coworker, you'll have a built-in pool of talented, motivated people who'll be interested in picking up your slack for pay or barter. Not only will your clients think you've developed super human powers because of how fast things get done, you'll gain major karma points in the coworking community.

CREATIVITY

Traditional business owners swear by "location, location, location." For coworkers, the mantra is "ideas, ideas, ideas." Writer's block, brain farts, and design paralysis are no match for a community of creatively-endowed people. If a problem project has you stymied, try shouting it out to the built-in focus group seated all around you (check to make sure they don't have their headphones in first). You might be surprised at how quickly you'll have more ideas than than ever.

WHAT IS COWORKING?

WHAT COWORKING BRINGS TO THE COMMUNITY TABLE

The following section (ending with "The Workforce Diversifies") was originally published by Shareable.net and is reprinted with permission.

Coworking does a lot for the people who participate in it, but let's face it, not everyone can be a coworker. We still need butchers, bakers, and candlestick makers with traditional storefronts to make our world go 'round. One of the most exciting parts about the coworking movement is that the benefits don't just stay all bottled up inside the individual spaces. They overflow into the local, physical community as well, proving that when we incorporate sharing into all aspects of our lives, it's almost always for the win.

FAMILIES STAY STABLE

In an economy in which 40 percent of all workers are predicted to be freelance by 2020, many former office workers have been forced to get creative when it comes to maintaining a steady source of income. Even those who are still employed often find side clients to supplement cut salaries or help them save for vacation. In the First Global Coworking Survey, published

"42 percent of respondents reported earning more money after joining a coworking space."

- 2010 Global Coworking Survey, published by Deskmag

in 2010, nearly half of respondents said coworking provided a boost to their monthly income. Regular money coming in the door means utility bills get paid, mortgages stay (somewhat) up-to-date, and families stay happy. See this link for survey details: http://bit.ly/1MaLWfq.

LOCAL BUSINESS GETS A BOOST

A coworking space provides much-needed structure for an otherwise dynamic (and often invisible) community of independent professionals. And there is strength in numbers. A large enough coworking facility can explore the possibility of group health insurance, sponsor speakers, host conferences, and offer classes: all of which draws people into the community and benefits the local economy. Coworkers who travel to coffee shops or lunch spots en masse can arrange frequent buyer discounts or barter an exchange program that prevents freelancers from hogging the tables all day. Win-win situations: they're a coworking specialty.

(AND STAYS LOCAL)

With outsourcing on the rise (both online and in the brick-and-mortar world), many small businesses find it hard to compete with the rock-bottom prices of an international freelance scene. When you bring independent professionals together in a coworking community they often take advantage of the immediate talent pool to delegate work. Instead of looking online to hire a developer in India who will work for $6 an hour, Mindy the project manager can instead suggest that her company hire Matt, a developer who sits two chairs over from her three days a week. The income stays in the local economy and the client gets a far superior website; all because of coworking. See "Five Ways Coworking Could Save Your Small Business" at http://bit.ly/2xC87LW.

THE WORKFORCE DIVERSIFIES

An unemployed adult with a severely limited skill-set is one of the most frustrating and heartbreaking things to see in a down economy. Focusing on one job all your life might make you really

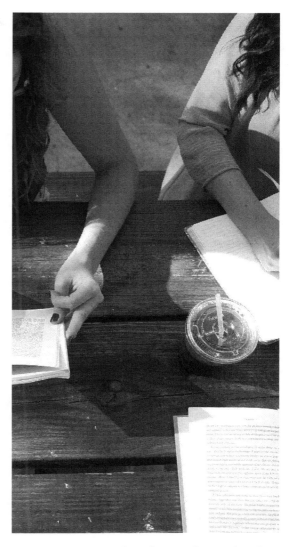

good at a couple of specific tasks, but what will you do if the company closes and that position disappears tomorrow? Independent professionals are adept at wearing many hats. They have to be, or they won't eat. Entrepreneurs and freelancers are constantly looking for ways to build expertise in new areas, expand their skill set, or add to their service offerings. Coworking gives them the safety and support they need to try new things, and the community is enriched by residents who are stable and more likely to be successful.

Right now, you're probably feeling very excited about the idea of coworking. It's possible that you're even thinking to yourself "this is what I'm supposed to do!" or "where has this been all my life?!" These are common reactions of relief that every person who learns about coworking has expressed at one time or another.

If you are feeling especially fluttery inside, thinking things like, "My city needs this!" you might be a coworking space catalyst. Read on. Pulling from my own years of experience, the following sections will teach you how to harness that energy and satiate your desire to "build community."

WHO CAN START A COWORKING SPACE?

"To be a coworking space catalyst, you need to possess the rare combination of altruism, community commitment, innovativeness and complete and utter bonkiness! Coworking spaces aren't for the timid. They are hard work, often unrewarded...But above all else, coworking spaces are intensely important for the community of digital nomads, freelance writers, startup entrepreneurs and independent consultants who would otherwise be sipping half-cold overpriced lattes in a local coffee shop, wondering the whereabouts of their birds of a feather. Coworking space catalysts are the ones who sat there one day and said, 'It doesn't have to be this way' and then put themselves on the line to make it happen. I applaud every single one of them. They are the backbone to this amazing worldwide community."

- Tara Hunt

President, Truly Social and Cofounder of Citizen Space

WHY DO WE NEED SPACE CATALYSTS?

If independent professionals knew how or why to organize for mutual support, they would already be doing it. And to

some extent they do: they may phone a friend from a coffee shop or attend every professional event in a 30 mile radius to solve their pressing desire for community. But these are only short-term solutions.

Inside every independent professional, there's a little bit of an introvert. This isn't to say that they find all public functions taxing--but in a small way, they've decided they'd rather go it alone. Maybe it's because they believe they're more productive alone, or feel like traditional jobs keep them from maintaining the right work life balance. Either way, there's just something that makes them happier when they're on their own. While this independence is exhilarating at first, it often fades into isolation after a prolonged period of time.

Despite its many disadvantages, a structured workplace does have one redeeming quality: it forces us to have daily interactions with other humans. Traditional coworkers help us get things done and distract us when there's nothing to do. When people leave the traditional office setting, they often develop this false idea that independence means they have to do it all on their own.

Picture this: because you're so focused on your work, you start to attend fewer events, which means you'll have fewer opportunities to connect with other professionals, which means you'll eventually know fewer people...which means you'll get invited to fewer things... see where this is headed? Self-induced pressure convinces independent workers that productivity can't happen if someone else is around. This vicious cycle is why independents usually can't (or won't) build a community all by themselves.

Unless entrepreneurs, remote employees, and freelancers actively work at maintaining a social life, there comes a time when they look up from their laptops and realize they haven't spoken to anyone in days. They may realize this is a problem--but they simply don't know how to reconnect without a built-in circle of coworkers.

Coworking provides a way to be independent while encouraging vital human connections, but just finding a room with desks and internet won't cut it. Someone MUST step forward to establish a place where productivity and a saturated sense of community can be enjoyed at any time, and that someone is the coworking catalyst. In a coworking community, the catalyst prepares and holds the space so that no attention needs to be paid to the environment, and instead attention can be paid to each other and the work.

WHAT ARE KEY CHARACTERISTICS OF A SUCCESSFUL COWORKING CATALYST?

The spectrum of personalities that start and run coworking spaces is vast. At the very least, a successful space catalyst must be a good connector of both people and things.

Every entrepreneur, including a space catalyst, also needs to be comfortable with uncertainty. If the idea of not knowing exactly where your coworking community will be in three months, six months or a year terrifies you, you may want to seek out a business partner who can balance your aversion to risk.

A coworking space catalyst should also be comfortable with and socially capable of being the face of a company that many people may not understand (coworking is a new concept for many). A space catalyst's time is consumed with the task of educating people about what coworking is, so it's necessary that they have the energy to explain the purpose of the business over and over again. With a smile.

Catalysts who envision themselves being a daily fixture in the community should have the ability and patience to help people get through barriers, overcome roadblocks, and examine the larger context of what they're doing in the world. People will be drawn to join your community if they can see and feel that each member is supported, challenged, and supplied with resources that propel them toward their goals.

Coworking catalysts should also possess solid business and financial skills, decision-making skills, the ability to be an evangelist for the coworking values/movement, and the ability to become personally invested in the success of members (it's the main KPI of any coworking space). If they don't have this knowledge, they should be willing to learn. Quickly. A typical Small Business Development Center in your city may offer the nuts and bolts of what you need to run the organizational side of things, like courses on business planning, financial metrics and tools, legal and tax requirements as well as how to structure your business entity. Unless you're sitting on a business degree, it is highly recommended that you take these basic and inexpensive courses (they're available online, too). The IRS hates it when you claim ignorance!

JOURNAL ASSIGNMENT

List 10 of your very best qualities. Do they correspond to the essential qualities of a coworking space catalyst? If you are having trouble thinking of them, ask your friends!

CHAPTER 1: THE BACKSTORY: ESSENTIAL READINGS & RESOURCES

ANGEL KWIATKOWSKI

THE BACKSTORY:
ESSENTIAL READINGS & RESOURCES

GLOBAL COWORKING COMMUNITY RESOURCES

Coworking is a state of mind, a unique global movement, and--most importantly--a community. This section will introduce you to the essential resources, readings, and seasoned experts you'll need to plug into it successfully.

Your first stop should be coworking.com. This amazing resource is crowdfunded and mostly run by volunteers who are passionate about coworking.

Here are the highlights of you'll find at coworking.com:

THE GLOBAL COWORKING BLOG

At blog.coworking.com, you'll find blog posts written by space catalysts, coworking community managers, and coworking enthusiasts all over the world. Many posts discuss tips and tricks for finding success in the amazing world of coworking. Achievements, announcements, and industry research can also be found on the Global Coworking Blog.

THE COWORKING GOOGLE GROUP

This informal group, http://groups.google.com/group/coworking?pli=1 acts as a support structure and discussion network for people interested in coworking on any

level: catalyst, space owner, or coworking community member. You're welcome to lurk here, learning silently from the knowledge and questions of others, but it's a much better resource if you introduce yourself and participate in the discussion.

THE COWORKING LEADERSHIP SLACK CHANNEL

The Coworking Leadership Slack Channel, http://opencoworking.org/news/projects/the-coworking-leadership-slack-channel/ is one of the newest resources available for those interested in becoming space catalysts. The Channel is filled with the most active and experienced leaders in the coworking world, and it's a great way to find immediate connection with other people who are starting and running coworking spaces. The channel is easy to join and there are always volunteer opportunities available for those who might like to participate as a moderator.

THE COWORKING WIKI

If you're looking for a place to cowork while traveling, or are interested in simply watching and supporting the growth of the movement, this is the resource for you. Successful business models, best practices, and hundreds of pages of user-generated knowledge can be found on the Wiki, http://wiki.coworking.org, as well as information about the Coworking Visa Program, http://wiki.coworking.com/CoworkingVisa, and space directory, http://wiki.coworking.com/Directory.

LOCAL COWORKING ALLIANCES

Many regions have developed alliances between local coworking and collaborative spaces. This has been called "meta-coworking" in that coworking communities are choosing to collaborate and share resources instead of competing. I have started an alliance in my town and you can see more about it here: focoworks.com. Use Google to find out if your town or region already has a coworking alliance.

Homework Assignment:

Find out if there's a coworking alliance in your area. Reach out to your local alliance right away and introduce yourself. They will be an incredible repository of support and knowledge for you moving forward.

THE FIVE VALUES OF COWORKING

Next, I'd like you to take a deep dive into the Five Values of coworking. Time spent reading about these global values will introduce you to our common vocabulary so you can "speak the language" of coworking and feel confident moving forward with your community building efforts.

These values should be the foundation and motivation for forming any coworking community. They are principles that can guide your decisions about where to open, how to operate on a daily basis, and how to market your efforts. But beware: if you were hoping to just copy and paste them into the About Page of your website and be done with it, you should know that the values don't come with explicit definitions.

The Five Values are purposefully vague and open to individual interpretation. You'll see some coworking communities interpret "openness" to mean no doors or walls, while others take it to mean all members should be privy to the business' financial status. The same thing goes for "sustainability" and "accessibility." Ultimately, you and your members will have to decide which interpretations are most relevant for your community.

To get you started, here's a walk-through of a few ways the Five Values can be applied. Think about which interpretation is right for you and your space, and be prepared to provide the community with an explanation of your definition. This will help attract people who are dedicated to similar values, and facilitate the formation of a happy, helpful community.

Coworking.com has a page devoted to a discussion of the Five Values: blog.coworking.com/core-values.

In my coworking community, these values have morphed into the following statements which are displayed on our Cobot signup page and on our website.

How to BElong to Our Community:

BE yearning for interaction

BE willing to introduce yourself, make friends, and help

BE ready to participate in both impromptu and planned events

BE eager to help everyone feel proud of our space and the people in it

BE prepared for abundance (work, laughter, goodwill, and more)

Here is my take on the Five Values:

COLLABORATION: This value is probably the most tidy of all the coworking values. There's not much to interpret here. Basically, it boils down to "a willingness to cooperate with others to create shared value."

COMMUNITY: This one has to do with the intangible benefits of coworking. In general, you'll find it referred to as a group of people with a shared purpose who both contribute to and benefit from the coworking environment.

SUSTAINABILITY: This word has been confusing ever since corporate social responsibility became a popular marketing tactic. You'll find references to financial sustainability, or the idea that all things must be sustained by the community. My interpretation is "do good to do well and make an effort to offset the environmental footprint of your space."

OPENNESS: This value often overlaps with the value of collaboration, particularly because it revolves around the free exchange of ideas, information, and people.

ACCESSIBILITY: This value spans the continuum of being financially accessible for members as well as physical accessibility. It can also mean that coworking promotes diversity.

JOURNAL ASSIGNMENT

Let's work on your interpretation of the coworking values!

What does Collaboration mean to you?

What role does the owner of the coworking space play in Community?

Why is Sustainability important for coworking?

How will your community and space foster Accessibility?

Can you truly be Open? How?

OTHER RESOURCES

MY EBOOK COWORKING: HOW FREELANCERS ESCAPE THE COFFEE SHOP OFFICE AND TALES OF COMMUNITY FROM AROUND THE WORLD.

While this book is targeted at your future members, it's an excellent way to step into the shoes of a freelancer, consultant, or remote worker. By reading this book you'll better understand every pain point that your future members are experiencing. Get it: coherecommunity.com/shop/coworkers

JOIN THE COWORKING CONTENT ALLIANCE GROUP ON FACEBOOK:

for any coworking operator who creates content.
www.facebook.com/groups/coworkingcontentalliance/

JOIN THE WOMEN WHO COWORK GROUP ON FACEBOOK:

for women who own or operate coworking spaces worldwide.
www.facebook.com/groups/womenwhocowork/

BUY A TICKET TO THE NEXT GLOBAL COWORKING UNCONFERENCE CONFERENCE (GCUC):

this amazing coworking-centric conference happens in a different location every year, and is the perfect place to meet like-minded people, learn from experienced veterans of coworking, and gather up enough inspiration to launch your own community like a rocket. Learn more: gcuc.co.

READ THE LATEST DESKMAG.COM SURVEY RESULTS ON THE COWORKING INDUSTRY.

It'll give you snapshots of profitability, global growth projections, and lots and lots of statistics! See six years of survey results (and counting) here: www.deskmag.com/en/coworking-statistics-all-results-of-the-global-coworking-survey-research-studies-948.

READ THE COWORKING HANDBOOK BY RAMON SUAREZ.

It's easily found by searching on Amazon. Ramon's book is a treasure trove of information about everything from design and marketing, to facilitating member connections.

**BONUS POINTS!
ATTEND THE VIRTUAL PEOPLE AT WORK SUMMIT.**

This incredible worldwide event transcends coworking as we know it today. It's run by the team at the world famous IndyHall coworking community in Philadelphia, PA. Learn more at: peopleatworksummit.com.

JOURNAL ASSIGNMENT

By now, your insides should be aflame with the passion and excitement that is coworking, so let's take a writing break before you go on your very first coworking field trip.

SET A TIMER FOR 5 MINUTES

In Column 1, list all the pain points your future members are currently experiencing at home or at the coffee shop.

RESET YOUR TIMER FOR 5 MINUTES

In Column 2, list a benefit of coworking that corresponds to (i.e. solves) that pain point.

COLUMN 1

COLUMN 2

Matching pain points with benefits will provide you with all the speaking points, content inspiration, and tour fodder that you'll ever need going forward.

"Solve. Their. Pain. Nothing else matters"

FIELD RESEARCH

Hey there future coworking space catalyst! Ready for some bona fide market research?

Your first stop is a coffee shop. I know. It feels like you're regressing a little now that you know about coworking, but it'll be worth it, I promise.

Field Research: Homework

Work from a coffee shop for ONE ENTIRE DAY or at least six hours. Why six hours? Because that's longer than any laptop battery lasts and I need you to feel all the pain of coffee shop working, including the panicked hunt for an electrical outlet. Do NOT reschedule your meetings or phone calls. Again because of the pain. I need you to truly experience how awful it's going to be when you're talking to someone and the barista fires up the grinder.

There's one more reason I have everyone work from the coffee shop for a whole day. The data you collect will feed directly into your future pricing levels. See the Membership Pricing document in the Appendix for your reference.

Buy a refillable cup of coffee and record the cost here:

$ [ ]

Buy a nice pastry or breakfast sandwich/burrito and record the cost here:

$ [ ]

Buy a fancier drink like a medium latte or chai or hot chocolate and record the cost here:

$ [ ]

Record the cost of anything else you bought:

$ [ ]

$ [ ]

$ [ ]

Total Cost of working at the "free" coffee shop for a day:

$ [ ]

✱ Now that you've had 20 or so ounces of coffee, you can forget about bathroom breaks. You probably won't trust your neighbors so you'll have to pack up your belongings and risk losing your choice table every time you have to pee. More pain.

Your total cost is about what a 1 day/week membership should cost.

Example: if you spent $15 at the coffee shop, your 1 day/week membership will cost ($15 x 4 weeks) = $60/month.

JOURNAL ASSIGNMENT

If there are other coworking spaces in your town or neighborhood go visit them and work for a day! I recommend going to three or more. Record your experiences in the space provided!

COWORKING SPACE #1 NAME:

WEBSITE:

What did you absolutely love about your experience? This can be anything from the website to how the rugs looked. Pay special attention to how you were "onboarded." Did it feel personal or special? Did they solve any of your pain points during the tour? Who did you meet today that you loved?

What didn't resonate with you about your experience here? These can be things that gave you pause, left you with lingering questions, or even made you uncomfortable. I'll never forget the coworking space I visited seven years ago that had hand towels so dirty they were black with dirt. Shudder!

JOURNAL ASSIGNMENT

COWORKING SPACE #2 NAME:

WEBSITE:

What did you absolutely love about your experience? This can be anything from the website to how the rugs looked. Pay special attention to how you were "on-boarded." Did it feel personal or special? Did they solve any of your pain points during the tour? Who did you meet today that you loved?

What didn't resonate with you about your experience here? These can be things that gave you pause, left you with lingering questions, or even made you uncomfortable.

JOURNAL ASSIGNMENT

COWORKING SPACE #3 NAME:

WEBSITE:

What did you absolutely love about your experience? This can be anything from the website to how the rugs looked. Pay special attention to how you were "onboarded." Did it feel personal or special? Did they solve any of your pain points during the tour? Who did you meet today that you loved?

What didn't resonate with you about your experience here? These can be things that gave you pause, left you with lingering questions, or even made you uncomfortable.

JOURNAL ASSIGNMENT

Bonus Question:

After you visit and spend the day working in several spaces, let's think about what was missing.

Were there any pain points that none of the spaces were able to solve for you? Maybe none of them allowed dogs, or were located near good restaurants, or offered fun events. Make a list of what was lacking. This list will become your niche. Whatever the other spaces can't offer, you CAN!

JOURNAL ASSIGNMENT

"An origin story is an account or backstory revealing how a character or group of people become a protagonist or antagonist, and adds to the overall study of a narrative, often giving reasons for their intentions."

—Wikipedia

Over the course of this workbook, I'll prompt you to write portions of your Origin Story. This story will be a powerful selling point of your coworking space, and one you'll tell over and over again as you meet people or give tours of your space after it opens. It pays to write down these musings and memories now so you can look back on them as the years pass.

What is your earliest memory of coworking? Did you read about it? Hear it from a friend? Not sure?

JOURNAL ASSIGNMENT

When did you first feel that coworking would be your destiny? Connect some dots here. Were you working for a company, did you suffer a trauma like I did and get fired from your dream job, or was it while reading this book? Record your struggle and why coworking resonated with you.

What has your own coworking journey been like? Did you join other spaces before deciding to open your own? Were there no spaces yet?

Is there a person who has already played a key role in your origin story? Maybe it's a best friend or your partner would desires you to stop working from your home office. Spotlight them!

Office Nomads | Seattle, Washington

www.officenomads.com

We are special because of the people. I know that's too easy of an answer but it's just the darned-tootin' truth. The Nomads are the greatest! Life is so much better with them in it.

"It is never too early to get your members involved! Be sure you are asking them for help, for input, and for support along the way. They won't disappoint you."

– Susan Evans, Founder

FOUNDING MEMBERS	*Zero. Whoops.*
DREAM TO GRAND OPENING	*7 months*

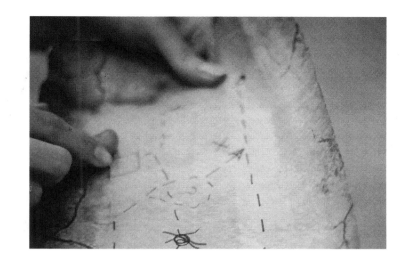

CHAPTER 2:
PLANTING A SMALL DIGITAL FLAG

ANGEL KWIATKOWSKI

SMALL FLAG; BIG LEAP

If you've gotten this far into this book (without skipping assignments!) you are probably ready to take your first BIG LEAP: declaring your intent to build a coworking community and thus planting a flag in the digital landscape. There may be a small amount of terror in your chest. This is normal. I choose to call that feeling "excitement" to trick my brain into continuing.

Why a small flag? Can't you just go sign a lease and buy furniture and people will flock to your amazing coworking space? No. Just no.

Starting with a very small flag on a very small digital plot has benefits. It costs very little and can be undone in a hurry if doesn't work.

ASSIGNMENT

Check off each "flag planting" item as you complete it.

- [ ] Name your budding community something straightforward and don't obsess over it for too long. I recommend Your City Name + Coworking. I started Cohere as "Fort Collins Coworking." If your city name + coworking is taken, find something equally boring that does the trick.

- [ ] Buy the domain for whatever name you came up with. I had www.fortcollinscoworking.com when I started. It later morphed into Cohere and **www.coherecommunity.com**, but that's a job for another day.

- [ ] Create a **www.MailChimp.com** or similar account for email marketing.

- [ ] Create a **www.Meetup.com** account as the place to host your events.

- [ ] Employ someone to set up a basic landing page on your new domain for cheap if you don't know how to do it yourself. You're not trying to build a state-of-the-art website, you simply need a place to point people, gather their email addresses, and identify the keyword searches that are bringing people to you organically. Important things you'll need on your simple landing site:

  - [ ] A definition of coworking/your take on the problem you'll be solving for your future members

- [ ] A blurb about yourself and why you're starting a coworking community

- [ ] A call to action to sign up for your email list

- [ ] A contact form or way to email you directly

- [ ] A link or announcement about your next event

- [ ] **A few pictures of people.** This can be your face at first, to be upgraded later with pictures of the people who come to your events

- [ ] Bonus points if you can publish a blog post every week but don't go there unless you can stay there. See also: the Facebook Group Coworking Content Alliance

- [ ] Introduce yourself on the Coworking Google Group with a link to your website

- [ ] Design/print 250 basic business cards with your website and contact email

- [ ] Write and deploy a short survey asking local freelancers, remote workers, consultants, entrepreneurs, and other people to tell you about their needs and desires for a shared space in your town. Capture their email addresses for your email marketing purposes

FILL IN THE BLANKS!

Name I chose for my baby coworking community:

Website I bought:

Meetup Group page link:

BUILDING A COMMUNITY: GETTING STARTED

PLANNING YOUR FIRST EVENT & GATHERING FEEDBACK

ATTENDANCE

Expect three to 15 people to attend your very first community meeting (Meetup.com keeps track of RSVPs). Even if only one person shows up, you can build a relationship with them and have them start helping you to spread the word.

SUPPLY CHECKLIST

☐ Name tags (nice touch, but not required)

☐ Large markers

☐ Self-stick easel pad or large roll of brown paper cut into big slices

☐ Your business cards with contact info

☐ Stats (optional: www.Deskmag.com has a printable card of coworking statistics that you can customize with your contact info and colors. Email carsten@deskmag.com and ask if you can have the file.)

VENUE

Any type of free venue will do. You can find a coffee shop with a meeting room, a community center, a church's recreation room, etc. It's best if the location of this meeting is roughly where you *think* your actual space will eventually be, but don't fret if you have no idea about location since your community should help drive that decision.

MEETING #1: 1-1.5 HOURS

Nothing fancy at the beginning. Introduce yourself as the meeting organizer and have everyone go around and introduce themselves. Ask a question like, *"What's your experience with coworking?"* Their answers will be gold and filled with useful info for you, the catalyst.

Explain what coworking is. The purpose of the first meeting should be to introduce people to the concept of coworking and educate them about what it means to live in a collaborative world.

Collaborative consumption is a way of thinking about how we use products and services. The main takeaway: sharing is the new owning. You can apply most of the principles of collaborative consumption to coworking.

Break into smaller groups or stay as one group if there less than six people.

Ask: What are some examples of people working collectively/collaboratively to get the goods and services that they need?

People might mention car/ride sharing, Community Supported Agriculture (CSAs), or their public library. Even a gym membership is a type of collaborative consumption because many people are provided with access to all the equipment instead of having to purchase their own sets.

This can be a free form discussion or they can write their examples on a flip chart.

Now, ask how collaborative consumption can happen in a coworking community beyond just sharing the physical space?

SHARE THIS!

if the group is stumped, share the following:

ONE OF THE MOST COMMON WAYS IS THE TRADING OF
SKILLS/EXPERTISE WITH ANOTHER MEMBER FOR MUTUAL BENEFIT.

Example #1	A graphic designer creates a logo in exchange for a fellow copywriter creating newsletter content.

ANOTHER WAY COLLABORATIVE CONSUMPTION HAPPENS
IN A COWORKING SPACE IS THE SHARING OF RESOURCES.

Example #2	Several coworkers may pool their collective buying power to get lower rates at a local gym.

COLLABORATIVE CONSUMPTION CAN ALSO MANIFEST ITSELF
IN COWORKING SPACES THROUGH THE FREE EXCHANGE OF IDEAS.

Example #3	While collaborative consumption focuses mostly on products and services, brainstorming and ideating are still valuable "commodities."

* Be sure to record all ideas, questions, and suggestions on your flip chart or big sheets of paper!

GOODBYE
UNTIL NEXT TIME!

Before they leave, ask people to share their contact info if they want to be kept informed of what's happening with your coworking plans. Let them know that in Meeting #2, they get to envision and drive the direction for the community!

At the end of EACH meeting, remind attendees that you need lots of help spreading the word, so they should be sure to tell their friends about coworking. Ask them for ideas on how you can spread the word about coworking in your town.

MEETING #2: 1 HOUR

INTRODUCTIONS *10 - 15 min*

Ask this question: *"What inspired you to come tonight?"*

RECAP *5 min*

Introduce the concept of coworking again: What it is, how it came about, and why you are passionate about it. Ask the group if they've ever heard of coworking and what they think about it. Recap the first meeting and even show the flip chart sheets with responses and questions from the previous meeting.

ACTIVITY *20 - 25 min*

Next, break out into small groups of three-ish people. Give them a big sheet of paper and markers, and ask them to describe or draw their ideal collaborative work space.

ACTIVITY *20 - 30 min*

Gather everyone back together and ask each group to share their work with everyone.

Leave at least 30 minutes for this because it will probably generate a lot of discussion!

GOODBYE
UNTIL NEXT TIME!

Inform the group of your intention to establish coworking "practice sessions." These are sometimes called "Jelly" sessions. Explain the purpose of a Jelly, and ask the group for suggestions on where and when to host it. See http://bit.ly/2fWXeKT for more info on Jelly sessions.

Collect email addresses.

JOURNAL ASSIGNMENT

Use the space below to write down how your first events went. Where was it, who attended (their names) and what you did as a group. How did you feel?

Idea: before hosting meetings deploy a simple survey via surveymonkey.com or Google Forms to gauge interest and gather feedback from the local community. Here's an example of a coworking pre-launch survey: http://denvercoworks.org/future-location-survey.

TIME TO JELLY!

Now that you have your small flag planted in on your small plot of digital land, you can host your first event! I think a Jelly is an excellent place to start.

WHAT IS JELLY?

"Jelly is a casual coworking event, where freelancers, home workers, and people running small businesses meet up in order to get out of their normal space, meet some new people and work together in a social environment. Jelly is a mixture of work, chat, comparing of ideas, passing on tips and help and maybe sometimes collaboration on the birth of a new project."

-Judy Heminsley, as quoted in Shareable at

http://bit.ly/2fWW0iE

Find a meeting room in a coffee shop or community space, and schedule your first four-hour Jelly event. Reminder: you are not trying to solve the world's problems in this first event. Your first foray into coworking events should feel like part mixer, part instructional video, and part question mark. Introduce yourself, introduce attendees to one another and ask one simple question, "What are you working on today?"

TIME TO JELLY!

Make a list of potential community spaces that would be good for small groups of people to practice coworking. The space needn't be fancy but WiFi and the ability to have drinks and snacks are key.

NAME	WEBSITE	COST

Have a Jelly one or two times/week for eight weeks. During these meetings, conversations about transitioning to a more permanent space will come naturally. Be a good listener!

JOURNAL ASSIGNMENT

What things are you hearing your community members talk about when it comes to:

Their desire to have
a more permanent place?

The benefits of
coworking for them?

Amenities
they want in a space?

Neighborhoods
they prefer?

Successes and wins they've
had as a result of your events?

Programming or events
they'd like to see?

FILL YOUR DANCE CARD

In addition to holding your own events, you're going to need to be out and about, spreading the news about coworking to your community in a big way.

Plan to be attending four to seven relevant meetings or events each week.

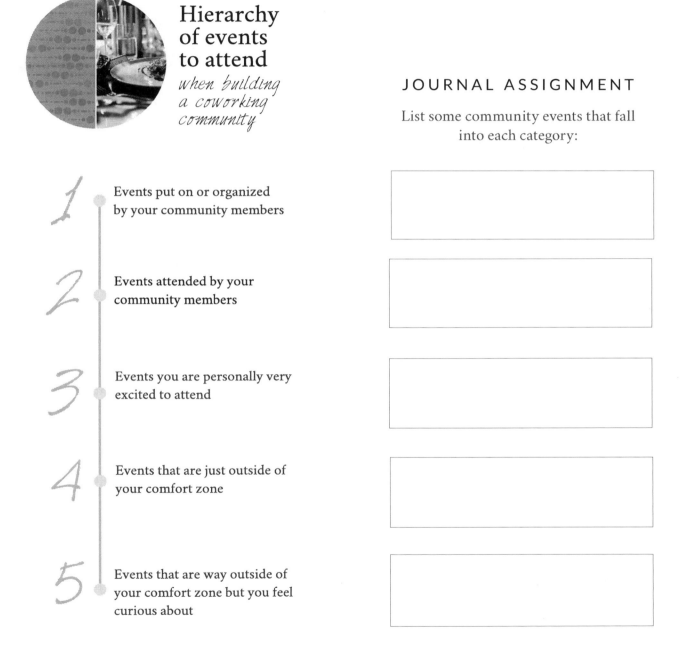

Hierarchy of events to attend
when building a coworking community

1 Events put on or organized by your community members

2 Events attended by your community members

3 Events you are personally very excited to attend

4 Events that are just outside of your comfort zone

5 Events that are way outside of your comfort zone but you feel curious about

JOURNAL ASSIGNMENT

List some community events that fall into each category:

JOURNAL ASSIGNMENT

Use the space below to write a short recap of each event that you attend. Include things like how the group made you feel, the general vibe of the event (happy, intense, technical), and the names of a few people you met with whom you'd like to reconnect with in a deeper way.

"Your Origin Story answers the question: Why did you start XYZ Coworking Space?"

Did you know there's *one single thing* that will form the basis of all of your coworking space marketing, content creation, and tours for the rest of your coworking community's life? I've owned and operated Cohere for over seven years, and even though I've used it over and over again, I've never told anyone what it is. UNTIL NOW.

If you're starting a coworking space right now, you're already creating this amazing thing. It's called "Your Origin Story" and I think it might be a coworking space catalyst's top secret weapon.

An honest and compelling origin story makes you memorable, relatable, and authentic, and if I've learned anything it's that people LOVE a good story.

My Origin Story starts with trauma, has plenty of twists and turns, and then shows how coworking changed my life. It starts like this, "Well, I had just been fired from what I thought was my dream

job and was adrift in the universe. I spent all of autumn reading the entire Harry Potter series under a blanket on my porch."

Do you want to hear the rest? I bet you do. Everyone loves a good train wreck and I had that in spades before I heard about coworking.

Before you do anything else, **write down your Origin Story**. It doesn't need to be comprehensive but you need to start recording the important details from Day One of your coworking business launch experience so you don't forget them later.

JOURNAL ASSIGNMENT

Answer these questions to develop your Origin Story:

What kind of pain were you in before you started coworking?

Where were you when you first learned about coworking?

How did you feel when you started researching coworking?

Who showed up to your first event? What did you talk about?

Why are you uniquely suited to have a coworking community?

If you've already opened: who are your founding members? Who stood by you as you started this crazy idea? What did you do on opening day? Who showed up? What was your favorite part?

Working Ensemble | Toronto, Canada
http://workingensemble.ca/

Working Ensemble offers childcare on site, so the community is linked together strongly by their experiences with their kids. Also, parents are awesome at supporting each other!

"Listen to your members and prospects, and adapt your system accordingly. Don't say yes to everything. Stay aligned with your values and goals."

– Diane Chevalard, Founder

FOUNDING MEMBERS	1
DREAM TO GRAND OPENING	5 months

CHAPTER 3: HOW WILL I KNOW IF IT'S (CO)WORKING?

ANGEL KWIATKOWSKI

HOW WILL I KNOW IF IT'S (CO)WORKING?

HOW DO YOU KNOW?

By now you've hosted and attended several events. You've collected some email addresses and made connections. "Is it coworking yet?!" you may be asking. Let's take a closer look.

I wish I could give you a tidy checklist of boxes you could tick and when the list is complete, you have a real, live coworking community. Unfortunately, it's never that easy. Still, there are some telltale signs that indicate that the community is truly starting to gel around you:

☐ People show up to your meetings and Jellies (even if it's only a couple)

☐ Someone brings a friend

☐ Someone offers to help you, whether it's by inviting others, hanging a flier, or sharing a post on social media AND THEY FOLLOW THROUGH. Be wary of the people who offer to help yet never actually do the thing they said they would do. Lots of people will think what you are doing is neat and people like to jump on neat boats, but they won't actually bail water if needed!

☐ You get calls or emails from people who attended asking when the next event is

☐ The group decides to make their gathering/Jelly a recurring event whether or not you can be there

☐ The group stays in touch online in between meetings via a Facebook group, text, or email

☐ You see strangers become friends and do things together outside of the coworking group

☐ You see members of the group interacting with each other in person or online and NOT discussing coworking

☐ You get emails from experienced coworkers who are traveling to your area to see if you are open yet (this means your small digital footprint is working!)

JOURNAL ASSIGNMENT

Jot down examples of the things (or the lack thereof) happening in your community in real time. This way you won't forget and fall victim to recency bias. Recency bias is when a good thing happens today and you can only remember the good thing that happened so you exaggerate how great things are going. Exaggerating the good things will lead you to premature lease signings before your community is ready.

_____

_____

_____

_____

_____

_____

_____

_____

_____

_____

_____

GET READY FOR THE ASK

After many weeks of test events and trial coworking sessions, take a head count. Are your numbers growing each week or have things slowed down? If you have somewhere around 20 people who are actively engaged in events it's time for the next step: Ask them for money.

I heard you gasp, so let's get real about this money thing. Starting a coworking business is a lot of work. While you can invest a lot of sweat and effort, you still need cash to pull it off. For small coworking spaces (around 1,000 sq. feet) you will need about $20,000 to start and that amount doubles with every additional 1,000 sq. feet. This $20,000 is not just for the things you'll need, it also offers you several months of rent while you build your revenue. So, don't go crazy at IKEA just yet.

If you feel squeamish about asking for money and worry that you'll never get over it, stop right now. You best find a coworking space to JOIN because the only thing that keeps new coworking spaces afloat financially is collecting payments every single month.

An exercise I do almost constantly with my friends revolves around the idea of how you value money and what money means to you. I think this is a critical introspective activity to do as you will often find yourself consumed with worry and anxiety about money now that it's your checkbook in the game. I solidified my thoughts around money when I was super poor after college and had a ton of debt. I read David Bach's book *Smart Women Finish Rich* (*https://www.amazon.com/Smart-Women-Finish-Rich-David-ebook/dp/B000SEH5BA/ref=sr_1_1?ie=UTF8&qid=1498184405&sr=8-1&keywords=smart+women+finish+rich*). There was a tiny little exercise in there about "What Money Does for You." I highly recommend reading the entire book, but I can also take you through a mini-version of it right now.

Draw a triangle/pyramid on a sheet of paper. Spoiler Alert: you're doing your own version of Maslow's Hierarchy of Needs. At the bottom of the pyramid write down what money got you today. Things like coffee, groceries, gas, a place to live... all your basics will probably spring to mind first.

Spend a moment pondering what you wrote down. Think about what it feels like when you have access to everything you listed. Now what does money get you? Write down these answers a little higher in the pyramid. You might have to press your brain and heart a little here. Maybe it gets you nicer food, a better house OR maybe it brings you peace of mind or allows you to be generous toward others.

Spend a moment pondering this new level. Think about how it feels when you have everything you listed. Now what does money get you? Write these answers a little higher on the pyramid. You'll have to press your heart even harder now. You're getting deeper into your values now. When your basic needs are met and you have a little extra to calm your mind, what does money get you?

Keep repeating these steps until arrive at Your Ultimate Value. Once you know what this deeply held value is, you can use it to guide all your decisions in life AND in your coworking community. This Ultimate Value is what you're seeking to provide through your coworking community. You should feel comfortable asking for money in exchange for what your coworking community provides, because your dedication to it enables others to earn money and pursue their own ultimate value.

JOURNAL ASSIGNMENT

Record your thoughts about the Ultimate value exercise in the space below. Where did you feel resistance? Where did you feel yielding? Were your brain and heart fighting? Why?

Write your Ultimate Value here:

_____

_____

_____

_____

_____

_____

_____

_____

_____

InSpark Coworking | Snohomish County, Washington

www.insparkcoworking.com

We are all coworking, no offices. Walls don't create community – and that is what's most important to me. It's been amazing seeing the collaboration and connecting that is happening already!

"People love to give me advice. I take note and trust my gut. I have to focus on our members first. Every other "should" idea is on the list, but not at the forefront."

– Tracey Warren, Founder

FOUNDING MEMBERS	5
DREAM TO GRAND OPENING	10 months

JOURNAL ASSIGNMENT

Go back and re-read Your Origin Story.
How might you weave your Ultimate Value into the story of how
and why your coworking community came into existence?

Angel's Ultimate Value

My Ultimate Value is Independence. I went through David Bach's exercise in 2001 while sitting on the bedroom floor in my brand new two-room apartment in Cheyenne, Wyoming.

I did the activity in pencil in case I messed up. I didn't mess up. When I wrote down Independence at the top of my pyramid it felt like lightning hit my heart but in all the best ways. I knew that if I had money it would allow me to be independent. That initially meant financial independence but as I grew and changed it would also guide the career path I would take, my deepest relationships, how mothering would be the greatest challenge of all, and how I would eventually work to gather all the seekers of independence in the world and create a coworking community.

My Origin Story includes the pain I felt when the CEO at my "dream job" told me that I was probably an entrepreneur and asked "Will you please go start your own company and get out of mine?" Knowing that my Ultimate Value was Independence helped me align my newfound unemployment with the burning desire to NEVER WORK FOR ANYONE ELSE'S PASSION EVER AGAIN. Seven months later, I would throw open the doors to Cohere.

Circling back around to the topic of money, whenever I feel squeamish about raising my prices or charging for this book you are reading, I remember that when I provide something of value to people, they pay me with money, and that money allows me to continue to be independent in my career, with my time, and in how I parent and show up for my family. So now let's talk about how to start selling for actual dollars.

THE NITTY GRITTY OF PRE-SALES

"I blame Kevin Costner for everything that's wrong with how most people approach starting a coworking business."

Now that you've overcome your (possible) aversion to asking for money, it's important to have a strategy for marketing your burgeoning community. I recommend that you start by selling a limited number of Founding Memberships.

You can do the same with smaller levels of membership as well for people who may not be able to afford so much all at once. Getting paying members in advance has the huge benefit of allowing you to open your doors with a bunch of people already in your space creating a vibe and having a great time getting their work done together.

In Field of Dreams, when Kevin Costner heard some voice in a field whisper "if you build it, they will come," he doomed many a coworking catalyst to failure. We are not luring ghosts to a meaningless sporting event. The metaphor doesn't translate.

Remember, the point of coworking is NOT the building, the desk or the WiFi. The point is the people and the pain you're solving is loneliness.

Shifting from a "build it and they will come" mindset to "community first, space second" will help you to build your coworking business on a much stronger foundation.

If you have **15 people willing to give you money** before you even have a permanent space, you can proceed to the world of finding a space!

"You can't solve someone's loneliness by inviting them to hang out in your empty building."

Hello Sam!

Our coworking community is really starting to thrive. Getting a permanent place for us to be awesome together is expensive. I would love your help to launch this thing together. I've made a little process so we can make progress!

You can pre-order a Founding Membership today. What does this mean? You'll get bragging rights for life and your first 6 months of coworking for 20% off the regular price. I can only do 10 of these. Wouldn't you like to be Founding Member #1?

Your Founding Membership Fee will go towards the cost of (list things like your 1st month's rent, lounge furniture, or sweet wifi access points, etc).

You can Venmo me the money right this second… or give me a check or hand me a fistful of cash next time we're together. I'd also love to hear your ideas on how we might spread the word about our community to a wider audience. Some super smart people have recommended over and over again that I have 10-15 people signed up prior to signing the lease to safeguard the community and my savings account. Together, we can crush this goal!

Love and Coworking,
Your Name

CHAPTER 4:
THE BUSINESS OF COMMUNITY

ANGEL KWIATKOWSKI

THE BUSINESS OF COMMUNITY

MAKING IT OFFICIAL

Even as you are building up your community through events and gathering membership pre-payments, you'll need to formalize your business per government rules. Follow this order of operations when it's time to transform that gleam in your eye into a full-fledged coworking business.

Disclaimer: I'm obviously not a lawyer or broker or doctor so none of my advice should be misconstrued as legal advice. Please consider hiring professionals if you feel confused, overwhelmed, or scared. I used a real lawyer to review my first lease.

1. Decide on a business name. This can be what you've been using (Coworking + Your City) or you can find your forever name. Double-check that the web domain and social media handles are available for whatever name you choose. This process will severely limit what names are available to you, but it will be better for marketing efforts down the road.

2. Decide on what type of organizational structure your business will have. Consult a lawyer if needed. I chose the basic LLC. It's easy to create and has some protections built in for you.

3. Apply to be an LLC by finding the application at your Secretary of State's website. It usually costs between $50-$200.

4. Apply for an **Employer Identification Number (EIN)** with the IRS.

Select electronic delivery if available, otherwise it takes about a week to get the letter with your tax number. www.irs.gov/businesses/small-businesses-self-employed/apply-for-an-employer-identification-number-ein-online

5. Go to your bank and open a business bank account. You will need your ID, Articles of Incorporation, and your new EIN.

Get a business checking account

Get a business debit card

If you are opening with an employee, you may want to authorize them to have a debit card as well. Your employee needs to come with you to the bank with their driver's license to do this.

Optional: savings account

Also Optional: drinking the free gross bank coffee.

6. Get business insurance by calling the company with whom you currently have car/home insurance. They will typically be able to get you a policy but may NOT be able to activate it until you have a signed lease with info on your square footage, sprinkler system, security system, etc. It's still a good idea to call and get a ballpark estimate of what your premiums will be. You can also shop around if you like. Be sure to explain plainly that it is a shared office space. They may have lots of questions. Answer them thoroughly.

7. If you are going to change your business name from Coworking + City, do the following:

Buy your new domain

Buy hosting for the new domain

Claim all of your social profiles: Twitter, Instagram, and a Facebook business page, for starters

8. Choose an accounting software. If you know you're going to use a membership management system, be sure that your accounting software integrates seamlessly with your coworking software. It will save you lots of time and stress in the future.

9. Begin to research coworking space management software companies. You may be able to get away without a software solution at the beginning, but I found that once you have 25+ members it becomes VERY hard to manage without a digital system in place. If your space is over 1,000 sq. feet, you will definitely have more than 25 members.

Here are some choices to look into: Cobot (www.cobot.me), Nexudus (coworking.nexudus.com/en), WUN (www.wunsystems.com) and EnsembleApp (ensembleapp.co). At the end of this section you'll find a worksheet to help you assess the different systems available to you so you can make an informed decision.

10. Choose a commercial realtor and have a meeting with them. Ask them about recent office space projects they have negotiated and ask to talk to some of their clients.

11. Begin to walk through neighborhoods that interest your community, and take note of the buildings and surrounding businesses.

12. Begin filling in the year Cash Flow Projection Worksheet in the Appendix. There are several tabs along the bottom designed for different membership capacities. You can play around with your membership levels, pricing, expenses and rent rate to see how the numbers change with different variables.

13. Design and order new basic business cards if needed.

Shecosystem Coworking + Wellness | Toronto, Canada

www.shecosystem.ca

We have created a container for women-identified people to really show up authentically in their work-lives and build relationships that go beyond networking. Shecosisters join for reasons other than work. For example, to celebrate engagements and be held while they grieve a loss, to organize for political marches, and to find support while they ride out difficult transitions.

"Attract your community by being very clear about the values and culture that you are trying to create. The number one thing people said before we had a space was that they felt like they had found their tribe - a group of like-minded people who united around shared vision and values. The space is secondary."

– Emily Rose Antflick, Founder

FOUNDING MEMBERS	*18*
DREAM TO GRAND OPENING	*14 months*

JOURNAL ASSIGNMENT

Choosing Coworking Management Software

Fill in the following sheet as you research the different coworking space management software choices. Compare them based on the following functions, which you you may or may not want your coworking software to handle for you.

_____

_____

_____

_____

_____

_____

_____

_____

_____

_____

JOURNAL ASSIGNMENT

	COBOT	NEXUDUS	WUN	ENSEMBLE	OTHER	OTHER	OTHER
Branded to your company							
Billing & Invoicing Automation							
CRM							
Multiple Admins							
Member Management							
Member Communication with You							
Internal Member Communication							
WiFi Access							
Phone Management							
Door Access							
Meeting Room Reservations							
Printer Management							
Sales & Membership Analytics							
Help Desk for Members							
Response Time from Company							
Monthly Fee							
Other							

Location Scouting

What neighborhoods/areas have your community members indicated they prefer?

Spend some time in the neighborhoods you've listed. Characteristics I like to look for in potential neighborhoods are: walking distance to coffee shops, proximity of a mail/copy/print store, restaurant options for lunches and happy hours, grocery store, hardware store, public transport, bike racks, ample and affordable parking options, safety of neighborhood at night, fitness centers, and drop-in daycare centers.

After you have visited several neighborhoods, ask your Realtor to send you some listings in your preferred areas. Ask them to also send you some "wild card" buildings. These can be non-traditional, unexpected, or unique buildings that don't work for other types of renters. With a small budget, you may also find yourself on the edge of cool neighborhoods but not quite in them. This can be a good thing. You get the advantage of lower rent but are still close enough to enjoy all the neat stuff nearby. Less trendy neighborhoods always have better parking. It's science!

Location 1

Location 2

JOURNAL ASSIGNMENT

Location 3

Location 4

Location 5

Location 6

CHAPTER 5: THE PHYSICAL SPACE, LEASES AND OTHER DELIGHTS

ANGEL KWIATKOWSKI

THE PHYSICAL SPACE, LEASES AND OTHER DELIGHTS

It's so easy... to jump in with both feet and sign a lease quickly. It feels exciting and fun and very rewarding, especially after all these months of digital research, meetings, and introspection. So many coworking catalysts sign a lease first and assume that people will flock to it, but as we've mentioned, this strategy often fails. "Lease it and they will come" can work in large urban areas where the concept of coworking is well-known, but most of you will start your first community in a smaller town or suburb where many residents haven't heard about coworking yet. Because of this lack of awareness, it's best to postpone lease signing until all the steps you read prior to this point are done.

Once you have an engaged group of people who are on-board and excited about building a coworking community with you (and also willing to pay), by all means, go huntin' for a space!

I could go on for days about what to look for in a building but the most important feedback will come directly from your current members. That being said, I recommend you do all the heavy lifting of looking at buildings and ruling out the worst ones by yourself until you have around three serious contenders.

Then, gather a small group of members and take them on a tour of each building. At the end of the tours, have them vote for their favorite anonymously on slips of paper and tally them up. Voila! A winner will likely emerge.

I poll my members constantly about everything. We're currently hammering out a new color scheme for our conference room and it's incredible. You can and should gather their honest feedback at every turn while preparing the physical space that will eventually hold them. Why guess what the community wants when you could just ask?

You can do all kinds of things in less-than-ideal spaces to make them quirky and lovely and fun, even if you don't have a truckload of money. Commercial real estate rentals are very different from residential rentals. In a residence you can expect your landlord to take care of stuff like plumbing, repairs, and having things cleaned and painted before you move in. This is NOT the case with commercial rentals. Building owners typically make commercial tenants pay for EVERYTHING from electricity to landscaping to paint, and some even go as far as requiring tenants to replace HVAC roof units that cost tens of thousands of dollars.

This is why I highly recommend hiring a commercial real estate agent. They can help you navigate the lingo and may have history with certain building owners, enabling them to point you in the right direction for no-hassle, reputable landlords.

Remember, even if you ask the landlord to paint and replace the carpet prior to your move-in they will likely prorate the cost of these improvements over the course of your lease so you will end up paying for it in the end. I have yet to find a landlord who is willing to pay for improvements. Even the nice ones. If you need to do a lot of build-out or construction, the safest scenario is probably to ask the landlord to cover the cost up front and then pay them back over time. This way if your business fails, you won't be on the hook for all those expensive upgrades.

LEASES: GROSS VS. NNN

When scouring real estate listings, you're going to see a lot of things like this "3,000 sq. foot $12/ft NNN." That NNN is like a giant freaking question mark. NNN or "triple net" is where the landlord puts any expense he can think of from your utilities to the property taxes and then you get to pay it. Your realtor can usually get the estimated NNN for a building but it can vary widely if property taxes change dramatically year over year.

That's why I've always pushed for Gross Leases. A gross lease is hard to get but it means that everything is bundled into the price and you don't have to worry about fluctuating taxes or utilities.

COMMERCIAL VS. RESIDENTIAL LEASES

Here is a list of characteristics that are *typically* important to coworking members but remember that this community you're building isn't about the space.

- [ ] Natural light
- [ ] Windows that open
- [ ] ADA access
- [ ] Large kitchen
- [ ] Stovetop/oven
- [ ] Conference room
- [ ] Phone rooms

- [ ] Good lighting
- [ ] Ability to change the light fixtures
- [ ] Level flooring
- [ ] Outdoor workspace
- [ ] Enough restrooms
- [ ] Interesting views from windows

- [ ] Walkable to coffee and food
- [ ] Changeable wall colors
- [ ] Open concept
- [ ] Nooks to hide in
- [ ] Window seats
- [ ] Weird architectural details

As soon as you sign the lease, contact your Internet Service Provider to schedule installation.

OTHER LEASE THINGS TO PAY ATTENTION TO

When you get the first draft of your lease, print it, grab a pen, and start editing.

KEY CONSIDERATIONS:

1. Repairs/Maintenance. Who pays for what when it breaks? Read the sections on electrical, plumbing, HVAC, landscape and janitorial. Run a scenario for each system in which the thing has broken. What is the required response time from the landlord and who will pay? Hint: fast response and a landlord who pays is the answer you want. For janitorial, if it's included in your rent, how often will the crew come and what happens if the service isn't satisfactory?

2. Renewals. Having renewal options is the best way to ensure that you can stay in your building at a reasonable rate over time. When you have a renewal option, you can stay in the building (but are not obligated to) and usually pay an "escalator percentage," which is a hike in your rent but way less risky than completely renegotiating your rent each year. For example, I am on a three year renewal right now with Cohere. My rent goes up 3.5% each year and then I don't have any more renewal options. My landlord and I will renegotiate 6 months before my final renewal is up. This will be a risky time for me as rent rates have skyrocketed in the past few years so I am bracing myself to see a significant increase.

3. Building Sale. Look for clauses that talk about what happens to your lease if the building owner decides to sell. Do you get to stay? Do you get a certain amount of time to find a new home? Check with a lawyer because towns/states can react differently to different sale situations.

4. Disasters. Read the lease sections about what happens if there is a fire, flood, hurricane, etc., very carefully. Think about how you would move forward if your building burned down. Pay attention to the time limits the landlord has to repair damages, if your lease stays intact, or if you can opt out in the event of a disaster. Discuss these scenarios with your insurance agent and find out what protections your insurance will provide to your business in the event of a catastrophe.

COMMERCIAL VS. RESIDENTIAL LEASES

5. Personal Guarantee. Talk with your lawyer and realtor about the personal guarantee section of your proposed lease. This is where you promise to pay the full amount of your lease no matter what. Make sure you are making an informed decision.

POST-LEASE SIGNING

I want to take a moment to congratulate you on your progress so far. You have spent tremendous amounts of effort building up a community, attending to a million details and probably lost at least a year's worth of sleep.

Congratulations!!

Go have a cocktail or absurdly expensive coffee. You deserve it!

Orange Coworking | Austin, Texas

www.orangecoworking.com

Synchronicity reigns! Our beautiful, weird, eclectic community runs on love and improbable coincidences.

"In the hustle of planning desks and square footage and cash flow, take some time to articulate your hopes and dreams for the community; for the humans who will be sharing their lives in your space. Really dive into it: what you hope your community grows into and brings into the world. Do you hope two people meet and fall in love at an event you host? Do you hope to have the next Google birthed with fuel from your coffee pot and collective wisdom? Do you intend to have a measurable positive impact on the economy of your neighborhood? Write it down. And re-read it every year."

– Shelley DeLayne, Founder

FOUNDING MEMBERS	*0*
DREAM TO GRAND OPENING	*11 months*

JOURNAL ASSIGNMENT

Continue your Origin Story

You've taken on a tremendous amount of risk by signing a lease for your community. Most coworking memberships wiwll be month to month so you'll bear the burden of significant financial stress until you begin to break even.

How does that make you feel? Who can you talk to about your feelings/ thoughts? How can you reframe any stress you might be feeling to align with your Ultimate Value?

_____

_____

_____

_____

_____

_____

_____

_____

_____

_____

CHAPTER 6: FURNISHING YOUR COWORKING SPACE: GETTING STARTED

ANGEL KWIATKOWSKI

FURNISHING YOUR COWORKING SPACE

Furnishing your coworking space is THE LARGEST expense you'll incur as you get going. It will cost thousands no matter how frugal you are and is likely to make you feel sweaty all over. This is normal and I'm here to help.

I've furnished FOUR different shared/coworking spaces over the years and boy have I screwed it up. From highly custom handbuilt curved workstations to bomb-proof college dorm desks, I've really put my members through the desk gauntlet and most times FAILED them. I've furnished spaces with uneven wood floors to carpeted floors to floors with lots of stains that required strategic rug placement. One floor was so uneven members couldn't stay pushed up to the desk on our rolling chairs. We joked that we should install carabiners to "clip in" for safety.

Here's just one example of a colossal furniture buying mistake. I drove 8 hours to Salt Lake City's IKEA only to come home with one-half of my office chairs in the wrong color. These white chairs provided lots of opportunities for Miami Vice jokes, and stupidly absorbed the denim dye from everyone's jeans so they looked old and dirty after approximately three days.

The important thing is that I learned from my mistakes and have finally found the right furniture for small coworking spaces. Rejoice because I did all the experimentation for you, and now you don't have to waste your precious money on screw ups like I did.

GENERAL TIPS

When it comes to the big stuff like desks and office chairs, RESIST the allure of Craigslist (unless you find the exact type of IKEA things I'm going to recommend, then by all means, have at it). Why? You'll likely never find matching items in the quantities you need, and when you grow and need more desks or chairs, you'll never be able to find more of that kind and you'll wind up in a coworking space that looks a little too garage sale-esque. (Hat tip to IndyHall in Philly who has to add a dozen desks every time they turn around, and luckily they chose a really common IKEA table/leg combo the store always carries. However, while their choice is the most economical one, it's not my choice since the tops can scratch and warp over time.)

I'm not a fan of prison-like uniformity in color/style throughout your entire space, but I am a fan of having 1-2 types of workstations and chairs, and then imprinting your unique style using plants, art, mirrors and pillows. This kind of 'matchiness' in large furniture makes it super easy to rearrange said furniture later and the room will always look pulled together no matter how you situate the desks.

WHY I RECOMMEND WHAT I RECOMMEND

COMFORT

Most of the large pieces are ideal because they just feel good. Whether it's adjustability or cushiness, don't ignore these recommendations. They are tried and true.

COST

Sometimes things just don't last forever. Lamps are one. They get a lot of action getting moved around and occasionally knocked over and they wear out. I expect a lamp to survive 3 years, so I never spend a ton on them.

FUNCTIONALITY

Most of the time, I just need something to do its job, whether that's holding hanging files for the business side of coworking or being so useful I can't live without them. See also: table top mount power strips.

NOTES ON THE LIST

CONFERENCE ROOM

I selected the BJURSTA extendable table because expandability is sexy, but another option would be to get 4 LINNMON tops in white with 16 KRILLE wheeled legs that will make it easy to reconfigure your conference room for different uses. The wheeled legs are way more expensive than the standard ones, but the thrill of reconfiguring a room with a quick push is priceless.

Pair your tables with the lightweight, stackable-yet-sturdy STOLJAN chairs. While I don't love the color combo that IKEA has right now, we snagged all black a couple of years ago and they are all still in service and comfy enough to cradle you for two-hour meetings or longer.

Below is a picture of the Virtual Reality at Night Coworking event we had a couple of months ago. Here you'll see we have the LINNMON/KRILLE tables with the STOLJAN chairs. That wall light in the background was an old IKEA purchase but they no longer sell it.

FILE CABINET

Be sure to pick up the ERIK I have listed as it holds hanging files, a MUST HAVE no matter how averse to paper files you are. Owning a business will have you running to Target for a box of hanging files faster than you can write labels for Lease, Insurance, and Furniture Manuals.

THE MAGICAL DESK CALLED THYGE

The THYGE is a marvel. They are sturdy AF, each leg is adjustable for uneven floors, and they slide over carpet with ease. The tabletop thickness lends itself perfectly to the SIGNUM power strip bracket so that power is always within every member's reach.

ADD A STANDING DESK OPTION

I recommend the HILVER bamboo top with GERTON silver adjustable legs. I recommend you get two sets of this standing desk and adjust one for taller members and one for shorter members. You know, equality and all.

OFFICE CHAIRS

Beware the online purveyor, Wayfair.com, for chairs. For whatever reason, that company is notorious for forgetting to include all the hardware, and you'll spend far too much time on the phone and waiting on the mail. I've had some experience putting together Wayfair-sourced chairs and those are some sad times for me. I prefer the affordable MILLBERGET office chairs because they are comfy, cost $69 each and last up to seven years or more.

SOFT SEATING

Sometimes you just want to go horizontal during your workday. I DIDN'T select a couch for you because the unique size/shape of your space would make it impossible for me to pick this out for you. However, I recently added a couch to Cohere and after applying Scotchgard liberally, it'll be coffee proof for 2 years!

I will recommend two POANG chairs in leather for you. I don't own any for Cohere but a member has one in his office and based on how often he naps in there, I think they are a solid choice. I chose leather so it resists stains (coffee and donut sprinkles), and the rocking version because ROCKING! Orient your two new chairs towards one another to create an extra quick meeting space, tea time spot for two members, or co-napping area. Pair your POANGS with the adorable leaf shaped LOVBACKEN side table so your members have a place to put their coffee and phones. We use the leaf tables at Cohere Bandwidth and they are awesome, though the bands tend to use them for beer not coffee.

ACCESSORIES AND CREATURE COMFORTS

Brace yourself and bring a friend for how much little stuff you'll need to pick up in the market area of IKEA.

From forks and bowls to coffee mugs, I've selected only what actually works in a real coworking space. Hint: buy extra forks and avoid the cheapest coffee mugs. They have narrow bases and are prone to tipping over.

PLANTS

Please find a way to bring live plants into your space. I chose a manageable three-tier planter and small pots for you to start with. You can do it! Cohere has 14 plants and we're doing fine. I prefer hanging planters to save precious floor space, but those are a little more advanced so feel free to add them in later.

LAMPS

I chose the same BOJA lamps we have at Cohere based on how many compliments we get. They look high end but cost only $59 each. They don't put off much usable

working light but create a soft warm glow that works well as evening approaches or rainy days.

COAT RACK

Provide members with the KNIPPE coat rack. It's sleek and has a small footprint, but can hold ALL THE JACKETS.

DESK MOUNTED POWER STRIPS

Don't skip these. They are a game changer, and they work best with the thickness of the THYGE table. Other spaces find the LINNMON tops are too thick to use the KOPPLA mounts. You can also daisy chain the power strips together even if you only have an outlet or two in your space. AND don't skip the SIGNUM under basket cord organizer. You only need one basket per two desks.

Above you can see the THYGE desks in action with desk top mounted power and IKEA office chairs. In the background is the standing desk (HILVER) I recommended above. The mirror was a gift from my mother in law. What I love most about this photo is it shows how absolutely messy coworkers are when they're at work. There are beers and travel mugs and water glasses. Extra monitors are everywhere as well as external peripherals like wireless mice, keyboards and chargers of every variety.

Messy is how real people cowork. This isn't stock photography where everyone is somehow being ultra productive with only a laptop and moleskin notebook. These are real coworking community members enjoying the space and each other during a night coworking session. Hoodies, hats, and love. Oh yeah, and sitting in a perfectly furnished space I

> *"Your community is more than the space that holds it."*

made for them using IKEA.

Ready to go shopping? You might want to split your IKEA trip in two just so you don't die. If you must travel far, rent a pull-behind U-Haul trailer. A 6'x8' trailer option should do the trick, or you can promise to buy your bestie with a truck ~~a plate~~ ALL of the meatballs once inside. And don't scrimp on dessert.

See the appendix for an IKEA shopping list.

IF YOU WANT TO START FROM SCRATCH INSTEAD OF GOING TO IKEA

Always remember that your community isn't actually there for the physical space. The physical space is merely the container that facilitates relationships. This very useful physical container does have some elements that we like to control and basic characteristics that coworkers tend to like, but your community is more than the space that holds it. Remember that.

VARIETY OF WORKSPACE OPTIONS

Some of your members will always sit at the same desk. They like routine. Others will pick a different desk or chair every day, or even move several times over the course of the day. Our job as space catalysts is to make sure there are a variety of seating and work surface options.

LIGHTING OPTIONS

Natural light is always preferable. It has been shown to improve mood and boost productivity in actual scientific studies! Try to avoid exposed light bulbs (i.e. the very hipster "Edison" bulbs) without diffusers or lights that beam an intense ray down on you (i.e. track lighting). You may be able to get away with these types of lighting in the lounge, entryways, or over a kitchen island, however. In general, pick something that has a diffuser or frosted underside to soften the lighting. Avoid fluorescent tube lighting whenever possible. It scrambles the brain! A surefire way to tell if your community hates the lighting is that they work in the dark. Pay attention and tweak as needed.

GATHERING SPACES (MEETING ROOMS/KITCHENS)

Meeting rooms with tables on wheels and stackable chairs are very useful. Some members might choose to work in the kitchen when they want to have extra social time with everyone.

PRIVATE SPACES

Giving members the option to hide away for phone calls or a moment of quiet is a nice perk that's appreciated by the entire community. A single phone booth is often enough for a 1200 sq. foot coworking space (more about phone booths in a minute). Members should have access to conference rooms as well to offer more private space without giving up too much community space.

COMFY SPACES

Make sure there are plenty of soft surfaces scattered around the space. Some members might find that they work best semi-reclined on some cushions or splayed on a couch.

RECEPTION SPACES

It's nice if reception is obvious as you enter the space. Providing lots of storage for staff is also helpful. I prefer when staff sit among the coworkers rather than acting as a human shield between the front doors and the people.

LOUNGE

I'm in favor of any piece of furniture that can be easily moved. While a large sectional sofa might seem nice, it could quickly get annoying if you have to move it around all the time. I like the idea of mixing in natural wood stools or tables accented with the bright pop of color offered by upholstered chairs. Lighting over the lounge should be soft and visually interesting. Whatever your team likes best.

ADJUSTABLE DESKS

If you are going to get adjustable desks, I would have them available for your permanent desk members. If you can find a desk system that has both traditional desks and adjustable desks in the same dimension, feel free to use a combo in the main coworking area.

KITCHEN

The bigger the better but if you only have a tiny one you'll survive it. Cohere's first kitchen had the approximate footprint of a port-o-potty and that's being generous. If you have the space, an island that has an overhang so members can put their legs under the counter while working is key. It'll be more comfortable. Bright lighting makes for easier chores in the kitchen, too.

PHONE BOOTHS

These can be pretty utilitarian. Having soft walls, carpet, and acoustic treatments will help with the quality of sound on conference calls and prevent noise pollution outside of the booth. My phone rooms each have a small desk, lamp, and swivel chair. Nothing fancy! I recommend one phone room per 800 sq. feet.

PERMANENT VS FLEX DESKS

I would keep these all of the same type/ dimension. It will make your life easier if you ever decide to rearrange furniture or repurpose a room for a different use. Again, 2' x 4' is a great size, and wheels are spectacular if you can get them in a locking version.

Make sure the surface of the desks is smooth. A recently-opened space I know of chose a textured desk surface and it's a nightmare. No one can use a mouse or write on a piece of paper!

COWORKING CHAIRS

Consider standard office chairs on wheels. They will be the most comfy for members over the course of a full day of work, and can be easily rolled around during events as needed.

LARGE MEETING ROOMS

A nice large table of any variety is good in a meeting room. I enjoy circular or oval tables if they work, however several small, matching rectangular tables can be configured easily. You could use stacking chairs or wheeled chairs in here. Stacking chairs are common in meeting rooms because more chairs can easily fit around a conference room table. I recommend one large conference room for spaces under 3,500 sq. feet.

SMALLER MEETING ROOMS

Ask your members what types of meetings they typically have. I've found that most freelancers and consultants meet with only one to three people at a time, if at all. A smaller meeting room is a better fit for these types of members, and doesn't feel so cavernous and empty while they are in there. A table that seats four and a whiteboard is plenty in terms of amenities.

LOCKERS

A great option for extreme weather climates where members will often be shedding a lot of outerwear or soggy jackets/boots.

THE SUN

Assess your space at different times of day. When the sun rises and sets, does it shine directly onto what will be work spaces? If so, find a shade or window treatment that can be pulled down. Avoid orienting your desks with coworkers' backs to the windows. The glare on their screens will drive them crazy.

PERSONAL STORAGE

I wouldn't provide anything for flex desk members. They can put things in their lockers or simply tuck laptop bags under their desk. For permanent desk members, a small filing cabinet should suffice for each person.

FLOORING

If possible, a soft surface like carpet tiles in the offices and under the coworking areas is essential. These surfaces provide a sound dampening effect in the space, and without them, every surface will reflect noise in every direction. Carpet tiles can be found in new fun colors and you can mix and match. I'd choose something with a print so stains and traffic patterns don't show, though it's fairly easy to swap out a soiled carpet tile.

ACOUSTICS

If your building has wood floors and bare/brick walls with exposed beams or high flat ceiling, your acoustics will be a challenge. Giant area rugs, canvas wall art, bookshelves filled with books, and/ or acoustic dampeners on the ceilings

JOURNAL ASSIGNMENT

Let's take a break from the monotony of space furnishing and think about things! Take a moment to dream a little about how you want your space to feel. Think about some places you've visited that you loved. What did you love about them? Was it a particular color, style, music or arrangement of items that spoke to you? Make quick list of style words and colors that you most want to see in your space.

Evolve Workplace | Minneapolis, MN

https://evolveworkplace.com/

We are special because of the mix of members we're encouraging to join/partner/collaborate with/barter among themselves. We also have a fully stocked gift-wrapping station!

"Start building interest in a coworking community the day you decide on a space. Don't be afraid to post a few construction updates on Instagram, or to push out tweets about your latest CraigsList bargain or trip to IKEA."

— Lisa Akinseye, Founder

FOUNDING MEMBERS   *13*

TIME TO TRANSITION FROM
TRADITIONAL OFFICE TO COWORKING COMMUNITY   *8 weeks*

CHAPTER 7: MARKETING

ANGEL KWIATKOWSKI

MARKETING

KEEP AT IT!

In between assembling furniture and comparing coffee pots, you'll need to do some serious marketing. Yes, you have a small, rabid following of founding members but you're going to need a lot more in the near future.

If I could only impart one thing to you about marketing, it would be:

Photograph everything!

For example:

- [ ] "Before" pictures of your space

- [ ] "After" pictures but only when people are there

- [ ] People at your events

- [ ] Selfies at IKEA

- [ ] Group photos, photos of your members, photos of people who visit, photos of events you attend outside of your space

MARKETING CHECKLIST

☐ If you aren't a strong writer, hire a ghostwriter. Secret: over half of the 400 blog posts on Cohere's website were written by Cohere member ghostwriters. Pro-tip: Ask around. You might have a blogger/member who would be willing to trade their wordsmithing skills for a discount on their membership.

☐ Download these printable content calendars and fill them out. Then, do the things on the calendar consistently and on schedule.

☐ Collect email addresses and provide useful, regular updates to your subscribers. See also: content calendar.

☐ Hire a professional graphic designer to design a logo, make several versions of said logo, and give you hex codes for your brand colors. I recommend having square and horizontal logo versions on a black background, a white background, and a transparent background.

☐ If you don't have the budget to keep a marketing agency on retainer, learn to use Canva or any of the many free online tools that will allow you to quickly and easily build Facebook headers, Instagram images, and email headers. Social media marketing will consume many of your hours, so you might as well produce good looking stuff.

☐ Adobe Spark Post is a free phone app I use to build Instagram posts on the fly while I'm traveling or waiting on appointments. I like this app because it suggests color schemes based on the photo you choose, so it's pretty fail-proof.

☐ In the early days, trade services for membership. This bartering (there's that sharing economy again!) gets you the things you desperately need while also filling up the space, so there is a positive vibe in place during tours and events. In fact, I still barter for web development and PR.

☐ Take advantage of paid boosting on Facebook so your posts will reach a wider audience. A $5-$10/boost is a good start and you can experiment with different types of posts to see what gets the best engagement.

Notable / *marketing resources*

CLICK TO EXPLORE!

1 COWORKING OUT LOUD
http://amzn.to/2wZ6SHe

by Cat Johnson

2 EBOMB MARKETING
http://bit.ly/2ycQt28

and anything else written by by
Amy Hoy and Alex Hillman

3 COSCHEDULE FREE
CONTENT CALENDAR
TEMPLATES
http://bit.ly/2ftC7iC

scroll down
to get the download link

JOURNAL ASSIGNMENT

Continue Your Origin Story

Look back over the things you've written in the Origin Story sections so far.
Start to stitch those together into a coherent narrative. Write that story here.

JOURNAL ASSIGNMENT

As you read through your Origin Story...

what themes do you notice? Is there struggle or triumph? What was the most pivotal point in your story so far? Perhaps it was something that happened, a person you met along the way, or a major lesson you learned. Take a moment to reflect on your Origin Story. How do you feel when you read your story? Write those details in the space below.

Cowork Waldo | Kansas City, KS
http://www.coworkwaldo.com/

We are a neighborhood coworking space situated right in the heart of the Waldo area. It's a place where "everybody knows your name". We're here to support and connect each other in our personal and business goals.

"Before you open make sure you have a solid business plan with multiple streams of revenue. Narrow down your target market and figure out where they are currently working. Sometimes you have to get out of your space to get people into your space, so go where they are. Build your community before you open your space as much as you can. And make sure you have at least 6 months of financial reserves in the bank to help during your startup phase."

-Melissa Saubers, Founder

FOUNDING MEMBERS	3
DREAM TO GRAND OPENING	4 months, 19 days

CHAPTER 8: THE FINAL COUNTDOWN TO LAUNCH (AKA THINGS GET CRAZY)

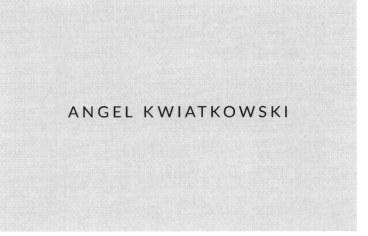

ANGEL KWIATKOWSKI

THE FINAL COUNTDOWN

Unfortunately at this point, you're at the place where there are just a bunch of random, final details that need doing and there is no right order. They simply need to be done before you can introduce your community to the world. Here they are.

PLAN YOUR LAUNCH PARTY

I'm actually not very good at throwing parties. I usually throw food and beer out on a nice tablecloth and plug in some music. I live in Fort Collins, Colorado, where jeans and a t-shirt is considered business casual. So we decided to have a cocktail party grand opening and everyone wore their smartest outfits. We had wine, cheese, chocolate, and snacks, and it was awesome. Later that year we wanted to dress up again for the holidays but decided the worst part of dressing up is the uncomfortable shoes so we all brought slippers to wear with our suits and dresses.

A really simple and non-traditional grand opening party idea is to have a potluck. Nothing says community like having everyone bring their best dish.

The most important thing you can do at your grand opening is have a **Membership Prize Giveaway**. Simply print up slips of paper to capture: name, email address and why they want to be a member. Choose one out of the hat and give them a free month of membership. I gave EVERYONE who entered the drawing a free membership for a month because WHY NOT? I had room to spare and wanted to make more friends. Almost every person who got a free month ended up joining and becoming long term members. One of those members is the editor of this book!

WRITER AND EDITOR BETH BUCZYNSKI

LAUNCH PARTY TIMING

The grand opening should take place about 30 to 45 days after you sign your lease/your lease starts. Your Launch Party can happen after you've quietly been open for a few weeks and have most of the kinks worked out. Six weeks out is the standard for large events so you have

ample time to spread the word and invite everyone.

BUILD HYPE WITH A FREE COWORKING WEEK/MONTH

Is there a general lack of awareness about coworking in your town? If so, I recommend offering at least a free week, if not a free month of coworking. This has several benefits:

- People get a chance to try it out risk-free

- It puts bodies in seats to amplify the vibe, connections, and energy in the space

- It allows people to feel the benefits of coworking even before you have a threshold of paying members

- You get to try your hand at community management from day one using real people!

Give people the opportunity to start paying even before the free month is up. If someone's been sitting at home waiting for you to open, don't deny them the gift of exchanging money for value as soon as they are ready.

ALL THE FINAL
THINGS CHECKLIST

- [ ] Finalize membership levels/pricing.

- [ ] Write membership agreement, send to legal counsel if needed.

- [ ] Create new member onboarding process.

- [ ] Write new member orientation document (see appendix for example).

- [ ] Buy Canon Selphie photo printer and 3M Command clips to create a fast member wall as people join.

- [ ] Hold a furniture assembly/cleanup day and ask your community to help you. Order pizza, get some drinks, and get IKEA wrench blisters. Together! Pro-tip: have your community members autograph the undersides of the desks to create awesome artifacts.

- [ ] Order/buy remaining supplies you'll need for opening day. Think coffee pot, coffee, tea, cream & sugar. Just the basics. Your space doesn't need to be 100% complete to cowork.

- [ ] Test and retest the WiFi and ethernet connections, if you will have them. Ask other people to connect their devices too.

- [ ] Finalize your business insurance.

- [ ] If you have employees, finalize your Worker's Comp Insurance, payroll process/ service, human resources paperwork/company, orient them, and make them build furniture and stock toilet paper!

- [ ] Fill in Emergency Action Plan Template (see appendix file for file).

ALL THE FINAL
THINGS CHECKLIST, CONTINUED

- [ ] Sign up for an Amazon Prime Business account.

- [ ] Order/buy basic paper supplies like toilet paper and paper towels.

- [ ] Buy/install accounting software.

- [ ] Finalize coworking software choice, begin setup process.

- [ ] Finalize graphic design for logo.

- [ ] Finalize website (see separate appendix for website dos and don'ts).

- [ ] Finalize Facebook Business Page sections.

- [ ] Finalize Instagram profile/pic.

- [ ] Finalize Twitter profile/pic.

- [ ] Advertise on Craigslist under Housing/Office & Commercial for each membership type/office.

- [ ] Create an event for Launch and invite people.

- [ ] Create an event for Furniture Assembly Day and invite people.

- [ ] Create events for any activities you already have planned: Donut Day, Waffle Day, Happy Hour, Lunch Out, etc.

- [ ] If offering individual mailing addresses, call your local post office for advice.

- [ ] If offering a printer, find a basic WiFi one ($100) until you know how much and what kind of printing your members will need.

JOURNAL ASSIGNMENT

Hey, you're probably open by now! Woohoo!!

How's it going so far? What's going really well for you and your community? Are you getting stuck anywhere? Write down your questions and post them in one of the many coworking resource groups mentioned early in this book (Google Group, Content Alliance, Women Who Cowork, etc.)

GIVING THE ULTIMATE COWORKING TOUR

The tour is the most powerful part of the membership pipeline. It's so powerful that I REQUIRE a tour be taken before a new member is allowed to join. How to give the right kind of tour--a tour that will demonstrate what your community is about and how it will benefit the freelancers, remote workers, and entrepreneurs that seek it out--is the the last and most valuable thing I can teach you before you strike out on your own. So no skipping over this section!

DROP-IN OR SCHEDULED?

I highly recommend that you take drop-ins when you first open and continue to do so until you are on a membership wait list, as well as giving people the option to make an appointment. Many communities will continue to take drop-ins but I opted to cancel that years ago in favor of having on-demand staffing. It saves us a lot of time and allows for a little prep time before each tour.

What you may not know is that the power of the tour starts BEFORE the person even gets to your threshold.

HERE IS HOW COHERE'S TOUR PROCESS WORKS:

1. Prospect fills out our online contact form at http://coherecommunity.com/ free-coworking-day-pass. You can see on the form that we "force" them into a few different times slots. This allows my community cultivators to work shorter

shifts and clump tours into groups. Each cultivator chooses their own availability and we list their name next to their time slot. This helps tourers see that a real human will meet them. We also ask the simple, open ended question on the contact form, "What brings you to Cohere?" In response, the prospective member will usually tell you their exact pain point, allowing you to solve that for them over and over again during the tour.

Notable
contact form responses

Here are some actual responses to our open-ended question.
Notice how all the pain points are laid out for you!?

 I started freelance writing full-time about six months ago (I'd been doing it part-time for about a year before that while holding down another job). I live in a tiny one-bedroom apartment and I'm getting cabin fever!

 I am a software developer that works remotely. I actually visited the midtown Cohere office a couple of years ago, but ended up not being able to make coworking work for me at that time. Things have changed a bit so I'm looking again, and would love to see the downtown space and meet some of the people.

 Hi. I'd love to check out Cohere as a possible part-time work location. I'm curious as to how flexible the part time option is as far as days and hours. I work occasionally from my company's headquarters in Boulder, and have my kids with me every other week, so I am not necessarily able to do regular days/hours, though in total I'm looking for about 20 hours a week on average, with some weeks less and some more. I would love to try dropping by early, like 8 am, if that's ever possible, because I'm already out and about at that time after taking kids to school... Thanks!

2. The chosen cultivator replies to the contact form/prospect to confirm the date and time. Here is an example:

Hi Lindsay,

I'm Jenny, a Community Cultivator here at Cohere. I am happy to give you a tour at 10:00 am next Wednesday, 6/14. We are located at 418 South Howes Street in a low red brick building. Park on the street and head down the south side of the building. Our door is labeled "Cohere" and you'll find your name and further instructions on the whiteboard just inside the door.

If you have trouble finding us or cannot make your tour, just call or text me at (970) 555-5555.

I'll see you next week!

Jenny

3. We also send the prospect a calendar invite with the address, instructions, and where to park.

4. On the day of the tour, the cultivator puts out a sandwich board to lead the prospect to our door, and writes their name and instructions on the whiteboard inside the front door. All of these steps are aimed at reducing the anxiety tourers often have about visiting new places. We've told them in two ways how to get there and where to go, and then guide them in like runway lights for an airplane. Also, people love seeing their name when they arrive.

COHERE'S TOUR PROCESS

WHERE MOST TOURS FALL SHORT

The tour answers a few obvious questions for prospective members: where to park, how to find the entrance, where the bathrooms are, how the desks work, and how to book a conference room. But you're missing a big chance to convert tourers to members if you just point these things out and move along.

CHECKLIST FOR TOUR LEADERS

- [ ] Introduce yourself
- [ ] Ask them how long they've been working from home or bring up something they said in their contact form
- [ ] Tell an anecdote about how you'll end their suffering or simply say, "We'll help you."
- [ ] Have them set their bags down during the tour. This shows that we care about them and that they can trust us enough to leave their stuff lying around
- [ ] Introduce the tourer to every present member by name. If they have something in common with a member, point that out. I've had to leave a member with a touree for 30 minutes before because I pointed out they were both into motorcycles. After their chat, pick back up with your tour

CHECKLIST FOR TOUR LEADERS, CONTINUED

 Explain the Where/What of things are but also the How, Why, When, Who? Tell a story. Here are some examples:

"Here is our printer"	V/S	"This is the basic B/W printer where Sara prints chapters from the sci-fi book she's writing and where Kim prints the protocol for the clinical trial she's designing."
"Here is our calendar"	V/S	"We have at least two social events every month. They are informal, low key and happen over here in the living room. Andy and Dexter like to eat lunch in here and this is where we have our Writer's weekly Cotivation group. Do you have to write for work? I'll hook you up with Chrysta to join the next round."
"Here is a conference room"	V/S	"This room is reservable so you can book it in advance for really long conference calls or to hold workshops in the evening. We've even had someone do a family reunion in here!"

CHECKLIST FOR TOUR LEADERS, CONTINUED

Hopefully you are starting to see the difference between pointing things out and telling a story.

☐ After they've seen the whole space and heard a dozen stories, we help the tourer find a spot to work and get on the WiFi.

☐ We don't do a hard sell. We like them to go home, think about Cohere or visit other coworking communities, and then opt in to us. Members who join quickly or try to skip the tour/free day are always the first to unjoin or leave without feeling connected.

☐ If they haven't joined after a week I email them and invite them to do so, or ask them if they joined a different community.

☐ If they join Cohere, we walk them through the Cobot signup process.

☐ Zapier automations send them a welcome email on their first day with orientation packet included.

☐ A cultivator is scheduled to meet them on their first day, re-tour if needed, and give them a real orientation packet that includes a Cohere sticker and Angel's business card.

☐ Zapier adds them to our Slack room and I add them to our private Facebook group. I introduce them in the group and ask an ice-breaker question like, "How do you take your coffee" or "Why did you join Cohere?" Current members typically comment and new connections are made!

☐ Print their picture and add it to the Newest Members whiteboard. After two weeks, I move their picture to the member wall.

COHERE'S TOUR PROCESS

Each time you give a tour, you'll figure out which aspects of our process work for your community and which don't. Slowly but surely, you'll work out your own tour process that introduces prospective members to the aspects of your coworking space that make it truly unique. Then, it's just a matter of "lather, rinse, repeat" until your space (and membership waiting list!) are full. Trust me, if you've focused on "community first" and kept your sights on your Ultimate Value while planning, gathering, and building a space for your coworking community, these lofty goals will eventually become reality.

JOURNAL ASSIGNMENT

Write the latest version of your Origin Story...

the version you'll share during your tours. How has your story changed since the
first time you wrote it down? What is most significant about your story?

Entrelac Coworking | Annemasse, France

http://entrelac.fr/en/

The Entrelac community is special because it's caring. We're going through a rough patch at the moment and everyone is rallying together to take us through this!

"It's never too early to start building a community. I wish I had focused on that earlier rather than thinking about space."

– Marion Majou, Founder

FOUNDING MEMBERS	0 at opening, 9 after a free week
DREAM TO GRAND OPENING	18 months

CONCLUSION

Well, catalyst, we've arrived at the end (or is it the beginning?) of this crazy entrepreneurial journey. You've gone from discovering coworking and having an incredible coworking dream all the way through to launching your first space. By now you should have a solid understanding of what it means to build community, ideas for ways to nurture the people in your space, and concrete tips and tricks for getting everything done. Through this journey you've written a memorable and relatable Origin Story, found your Ultimate Value, and done a lot of introspection (which is really hard work).

I sincerely hope that you and your community are beginning to thrive. Bringing people into and being a part of the giant global coworking community is a thing that brings me daily joy. I'm so delighted to call you a neighbor in this community and please know that I like you just the way you are. Happy coworking!

Love, Angel

APPENDIX: COWORKING RESOURCES & TEMPLATES

ANGEL KWIATKOWSKI

Amazing / *coworking resources!*

1 DIY MARKETING
RESEARCH:
MEMBERSHIP LEVELS
& PRICING
http://bit.ly/2yb6sxE

Tip! These files will prompt you to "Copy document." Click the "Make a copy" button to create and save an editable copy to Google Drive.

2 COWORKING
WEBSITE
DOS AND DON'TS
http://bit.ly/2xEyKh5

3 MEMBER
ORIENTATION
DOCUMENT
http://bit.ly/2xFBcE1

4 DIY EMERGENCY
ACTION PLAN
TEMPLATE
http://bit.ly/2wnDHJz

5 CASH FLOW
WORKSHEET
http://bit.ly/2fUvdnd

Author videos! View Angel's videos on everything from a tour of Cohere Coworking to her formula for a powerful and simple coworking event.

6 VIDEO:
MOST POWERFUL AND
SIMPLE COWORKING
EVENT (5:32)
http://bit.ly/2wnvIfE

7 VIDEO:
TOUR OF
COHERE (4:17)
http://bit.ly/2wZYgjB

8 VIDEO:
DIY EMERGENCY
PROCEDURES
CONFESSION (6:12)
http://bit.ly/2xPdPK7

9 VIDEO:
HOW TO MAKE A
DIY SANDWICH BOARD
(3:12)
http://bit.ly/2wXOsXw

10 VIDEO:
DIY MEMBER WALL
FOR COWORKING
SPACES (7:54)
http://bit.ly/2wmBMVy